ERICA BARRETT

Shuga & Seoul

A COLLECTION OF

SWEET AND SOULFUL RECIPES CREATED
FROM THE DEPTHS OF THE SOUTH

Shuga & Seoul

ERICA BARRETT

Photographs by Victor Protasio, Fratelli Studios and Erik Umphery

I dedicate this book to God, it is through him that I have been able to do my life's work. To my husband, mother, sister, grandma, family and close friends. Thank you all supporting me through my journey as an entrepreneur, chef and now author.

— Erica Barrett

FOREWORD

For the last 11 years, Erica Barrett has adopted several titles in my life; friend, sorority sister and mentor. But what she's most recognized for is being a rock star.

From conceptualizing the Southern Culture Empire, to the Erica Barrett brand, everything Erica touches turns to gold. This time, she does it with her very own cookbook, Shuga and Seoul.

Shuga and Seoul is the millennials foodies handbook to good eats. Erica's handcrafted treats and sweets are a reflection of the love she puts into the food, surely to keep any date night exciting.

Shuga and Seoul is more than just a cookbook. This compilation of tasty goodness has something for everyone. It's fun, easy to read, and will ignite the inner chef in anybody who can get their hands on it.

As an 11 year vegan, I too am able to recreate and indulge in Erica's recipes including my favorite, her vegan blueberry pancakes.

I am beyond proud of the energy that went into crafting this work of art. Erica's ability to translate her ideas into text speaks volumes to how passionate she is about southern cuisine. I mean, this girl can cook! And just as magical as Erica is in the kitchen, she is an extraordinarily impressive business woman. There is no doubt that Shuga and Seoul will be a staple item in every American household.

Erica, thank you for creating food WE can believe in, and being the genius that you are. You saw the need, created the demand, and now the ceiling has been shattered.

And just like you, this installment is sweet like Shuga with a whole lotta' Seoul. Now let's eat!

Aisha "Pinky" Cole
Founder, Slutty Vegan

TABLE OF CONTENTS

SHUGA

SEOUL

WHO AM I?

If I could use two words to describe me, I would use "Bama Girl." I'm Southern, I'm simple and I love to cook. My love for cooking came at an early age. I was about 9. I'm from a small town so there wasn't very much to do on weekends and summers, so I turned to my grandmother's cookbooks and Southern Living magazines. Those publications peaked my curiosity and led me to cooking breakfast and eventually dinner for my family. My mom and sister was so proud of my food, they would invite my aunts and friends to dinner on Sunday. I knew then that I found something I was good at. Meals would often consist of pork chops, fried chicken, lima beans, cabbage, scalloped potatoes and so many other comforting dishes.

At 17, I went away for college to Clark Atlanta University to major in Business Administration with a concentration in Finance. I had never considered becoming a chef at that point. I didn't know I could make a living from cooking, so I did what most kids would do... choose a profession and stick to it. Throughout school I partnered with friends and started to sell Sunday dinners to my classmates. Our Sunday dinners were a success but small dorm room kitchens we pretty difficult to cook for the masses so we stopped. The college years passed and soon it was time to graduate. I knew that one day I would own a business, but I couldn't figure out what business I wanted to start so I headed to Target Corporation for a management career.

Working at Target was great for me. I learned so much. I learned how to handle different personalities, manage crisis situations, branding, selling and even business budgeting. My years there gave me a launching pad for managing a business. Not to mention I made lifetime friends and won every single cooking contest amongst my colleagues. There was still a void, I made great money and was living the American dream. I had a nice condo in the city and a great career, but I didn't feel happy or fulfilled. I was offered a job at a payroll company and quickly accepted. I thought the career move was a fresh start.

I began my career at Paychex and absolutely loved it. I was now a HR consultant. I had a great salary, I scheduled my client meetings accordingly and learned a lot about managing people and creating great work environments. After working with Paychex, I was offered a job with ADP, their competitor. I knew as I continued my career in Human Resources, I would quickly climb the corporate ladder, but with no fulfillment. It was at ADP, that I started catering on weekends. My friends started to pay me to cook for their parties, baby showers and corporate gatherings. But one Saturday morning at the grocery store, had the idea to start a breakfast company. I named it Southern Culture.

Southern Culture was all about breakfast and Southern food. From fluffy pancakes and waffles to Fried Chicken and grits. I have been able to create products for the world to eat and a lot of recipes in the 6 years I have been in business. This book is my secret vault of my years experimenting in my kitchen and perfecting my craft. I hope that in every recipe you receive my love through food.

ERICA'S FAMOUS VANILLA BEAN PANCAKES AND WAFFLES

MAKES 4 SERVINGS

INGREDIENTS

- 2 cups all-purpose flour
- ½ teaspoon baking soda
- 1 teaspoon baking powder
- 2 tablespoons sugar
- ¼ teaspoon salt
- 1 teaspoon of good vanilla or vanilla bean paste
- 2 eggs
- 2 cups buttermilk
- 4 tablespoons of melted butter

INSTRUCTIONS

1. In a bowl, combine all -purpose flour, baking soda, baking powder, sugar and salt. Mix well together with a fork or whisk.

2. Heat an electric griddle or frying pan to 350° F.

3. Whisk together the egg whites and the buttermilk in a small bowl. In another bowl, whisk the egg yolks with the melted butter.

4. Combine the buttermilk mixture with the egg yolk mixture in a mixing bowl and whisk together until combined. Pour the liquid ingredients on top of the pancake mix. Using a whisk, mix the batter just enough to bring it together. Now fold in the vanilla. Don't try to work all the lumps out.

5. Lightly butter or grease the griddle and wipe off with a paper towel.

6. Gently ladle the pancake batter onto the griddle and sprinkle on fruit if desired. When bubbles begin to set around the edges of the pancake and the griddle-side of the cake is golden, gently flip the pancakes. Continue to cook 2 to 3 minutes or until the pancake is set.

7. For waffles, gently ladle mixture in waffle maker and cook for 2-3 minutes on each side or until golden brown.

LEMON BLUEBERRY PANCAKES

MAKES 4 SERVINGS

INGREDIENTS

- 2 cups all-purpose flour
- ½ teaspoon baking soda
- 1 teaspoon baking powder
- 2 tablespoons sugar
- ¼ teaspoon salt
- 1 lemon zested and juiced

- 1 cup fresh blueberries
- 1 teaspoon of good vanilla or vanilla bean paste
- 2 eggs
- 2 cups buttermilk
- 4 tablespoons of melted butter

INSTRUCTIONS

1. In a bowl, combine all-purpose flour, baking soda, baking powder, sugar and salt. Mix well together with a fork or whisk.

2. Add lemon juice and zest. Also add the blueberries. Mix well.

3. Heat an electric griddle or frying pan to 350° F.

4. Whisk together the egg whites and the buttermilk in a small bowl. In another bowl, whisk the egg yolks with the melted butter.

5. Combine the buttermilk mixture with the egg yolk mixture in a mixing bowl and whisk together until combined. Pour the liquid ingredients on top of the pancake mix. Using a whisk, mix the batter just enough to bring it together. Now fold in the vanilla. Don't try to work all the lumps out.

6. Lightly butter or grease the griddle and wipe off with a paper towel.

7. Gently ladle the pancake batter onto the griddle and sprinkle on fruit if desired. When bubbles begin to set around the edges of the pancake and the griddle -side of the cake is golden, gently flip the pancakes. Continue to cook 2 to 3 minutes or until the pancake is set.

8. For waffles, gently ladle mixture in waffle maker and cook for 2-3 minutes on each side or until golden brown.

RED VELVET WAFFLES

MAKES 4 SERVINGS

INGREDIENTS

- 2 cups all-purpose flour
- ½ teaspoon baking soda
- 1 teaspoon baking powder
- ¼ cup sugar
- ¼ cup baking cocoa
- ¼ teaspoon salt
- 3 tablespoons of red food coloring
- 1 teaspoon of good vanilla or vanilla bean paste
- 2 eggs
- 2 cups buttermilk
- 4 tablespoons of melted butter

INSTRUCTIONS

1. In a bowl, combine all-purpose flour, baking soda, baking powder, sugar, cocoa powder and salt. Mix well together with a fork or whisk.

2. Heat an electric griddle or frying pan to 350° F.

3. Whisk together the eggs, buttermilk and melted butter in a small bowl.

4. Pour the liquid ingredients on top of the dry ingredients. Using a whisk, mix the batter just enough to bring it together. Now fold in the vanilla and red food coloring.

5. Gently ladle the waffle batter onto the waffle maker. Cook 2 ½ minutes on each side.

BANANA WALNUT PANCAKES

MAKES 4 SERVINGS

INGREDIENTS

- 2 cups all-purpose flour
- ½ teaspoon baking soda
- 1 teaspoon baking powder
- 2 tablespoons sugar
- ¼ teaspoon salt
- ¼ cup walnuts
- 2 sliced bananas
- 1 teaspoon of good vanilla or vanilla bean paste
- 2 eggs
- 2 cups buttermilk
- 4 tablespoons of melted butter

INSTRUCTIONS

1. In a bowl, combine all -purpose flour, baking soda, baking powder, sugar and salt. Mix well together with a fork or whisk.

2. Heat an electric griddle or frying pan to 350° F.

3. Whisk together the egg whites and the buttermilk in a small bowl. In another bowl, whisk the egg yolks with the melted butter.

4. Combine the buttermilk mixture with the egg yolk mixture in a mixing bowl and whisk together until combined. Pour the liquid ingredients on top of the pancake mix. Using a whisk, mix the batter just enough to bring it together. Now fold in the vanilla, walnuts and bananas. Don't try to work all the lumps out.

5. Lightly butter or grease the griddle and wipe off with a paper towel.

6. Gently ladle the pancake batter onto the griddle and sprinkle on fruit if desired. When bubbles begin to set around the edges of the pancake and the griddle -side of the cake is golden, gently flip the pancakes. Continue to cook 2 to 3 minutes or until the pancake is set.

7. For waffles, gently ladle mixture in waffle maker and cook for 2-3 minutes on each side or until golden brown.

PANCAKE AND SAUSAGE DOGS

MAKES 6 SERVINGS

INGREDIENTS

- 12 breakfast sausage links, cooked
- 2 cups of Erica's Famous Vanilla Bean Pancakes (see page 3)
- 12 wooden skewers
- vegetable or canola oil, for frying

INSTRUCTIONS

1. Prepare the sausage links on the stovetop, according to the packaged directions. Drain and set aside.

2. Heat the vegetable oil in a heavy bottom pot over medium-high heat to 350° F.

3. In a large bowl, combine the pancake mix (follow recipe). Do not over-mix, lumps are good. Let stand 1-2 minutes to thicken. Transfer batter into a tall glass for dipping.

4. Insert a wooden skewer into each sausage link.

5. Dip the sausages into the pancake batter and allow any excess to drip off.

6. Carefully place in heated oil. After about 60-90 seconds, the skewer should float to the top. Turn to ensure it cooks on all sides.

7. Cook and additional minute to ensure outside is golden brown.

BLUEBERRY DOUGHNUT HOLES

MAKES 6 SERVINGS

INGREDIENTS

- vegetable oil for frying
- 2 cups all-purpose flour
- 3 tablespoons of sugar
- 1 tablespoon of baking powder
- 1 tsp salt
- ¼ cup fresh blueberries
- 5 tablespoons cold butter
- ¾ cups of milk

FOR ROLLING

- ¼ cup granulated sugar

INSTRUCTIONS

1. Combine flour, sugar, baking powder and salt and mix.

2. Using a pastry cutter or hands, cut butter into your flour mixture until it resembles coarse crumbs.

3. Add milk, fresh blueberries and mix until all ingredients are combined.

4. Transfer dough onto a well-floured surface, and knead gently until it forms a cohesive ball. If dough is too sticky to manage, continue to work in flour until it is smooth and manageable.

5. Break off approximately 1 ½ tbsp-sized pieces of dough and roll into smooth, tight balls. Set aside.

6. Fill a medium-sized saucepan 2-inches deep with your oil over medium-high heat.

7. Heat oil to 350° F (use a candy thermometer if you would like).

8. Prepare a plate for your cooked donut holes by lining them with paper towels.

9. Once oil has reached 350° F, very carefully fry your donut holes, about 4 at a time, carefully transferring them to the oil with a slotted spoon.

10. Prepare a sugar dish for rolling.

11. Fry donut holes for approximately 3.5 minutes, remove carefully with a slotted spoon, and place them on a paper towel laden plate. Allow doughnut hole to sit for about 30 seconds and then use another spoon to transfer them to your sugar dish, roll them in the topping until fully covered, and then transfer to your other paper towel lined plate.

12. Repeat until all donut holes are cooked and have been rolled in sugar.

MILLION DOLLAR FRENCH TOAST

MAKES 4 SERVINGS

INGREDIENTS

- 1 cup half-and-half
- 3 large eggs
- 3 tablespoons honey
- 3 tablespoons of sugar
- ¼ teaspoon salt
- 8 slices of brioche bread
- 4 tablespoons butter
- 1 pinch of cinnamon

INSTRUCTIONS

1. In medium size mixing bowl, whisk together the half-and-half, eggs, honey, sugar, salt and cinnamon. When ready to cook, pour mixture into a pie pan and set aside.

2. Preheat oven to 375° F. Dip bread into mixture, allow to soak for 30 seconds on each side, and then remove to a cooling rack that is sitting in a sheet pan, and allow to sit for 1 to 2 minutes.

3. Over medium-low heat, melt 1 tablespoon of butter in a 10-inch nonstick saute pan. Place 2 slices of bread at a time into the pan and cook until golden brown, approximately 2 to 3 minutes per side. Remove from pan and place on rack in oven for 5 minutes.

4. Repeat with all 8 slices. Serve immediately with maple syrup, whipped cream or fruit.

CANDIED BACON

MAKES 6 SERVINGS

INGREDIENTS

- 12 slices of bacon
- ½ cup light brown sugar
- 1 teaspoon cayenne pepper

INSTRUCTIONS

1. Preheat the oven to 325° F.
2. Place brown sugar and cayenne pepper in a large bowl and mix well.
3. Add bacon to bowl and cover each piece with coating.
4. Place on a baking sheet and lay bacon flat.
5. Place the tray in the center of the oven and bake for 15 minutes or until golden brown.

PRALINE PECAN CANDIED BACON

MAKES 6 SERVINGS

INGREDIENTS

- 12 slices of bacon
- ½ cup light brown sugar
- ¼ cup finely crushed pecans
- 1 teaspoon black pepper

INSTRUCTIONS

1. Preheat the oven to 325° F.
2. Place brown sugar, crushed pecans and black pepper in a large bowl and mix well.
3. Add bacon to bowl and cover each piece with coating.
4. Place on a baking sheet and lay bacon flat.
5. Place the tray in the center of the oven and bake for 15 minutes or until golden brown.

BIRTHDAY CAKE CUPCAKES

MAKES 12 SERVINGS

INGREDIENTS

CUPCAKES

- 3 tablespoons unsalted butter (room temperature)
- ⅓ cup vegetable oil
- 1 cup sugar
- 1 ½ teaspoons good vanilla extract
- 1 ⅓ cup + 1 tablespoon all-purpose flour (I prefer white lily)
- 1 ½ teaspoons baking powder
- ½ teaspoon salt
- ½ cup buttermilk room temperature
- 3 large egg whites room temperature
- ⅓ cup sprinkles

VANILLA BUTTERCREAM FROSTING

- 1 cup unsalted butter softened to room temperature
- ¼ teaspoon salt
- 3 cups powdered sugar
- 3 tablespoons heavy whipping cream
- 1 teaspoon good vanilla extract
- sprinkles

INSTRUCTIONS

CUPCAKES

1. Preheat oven to 350° F and prepare a 12 count muffin tin with paper liners. Set aside.
2. Place butter in the bowl of stand mixer (or you may use a large bowl and an electric hand mixer) and beat until nice and smooth.
3. Add sugar and oil and beat again until ingredients are very well-combined, smooth, and creamy.
4. Scrape down the sides and bottom of the bowl and then stir in your vanilla extract.
5. In a separate bowl, whisk together flour, baking powder, and salt.
6. With mixer on low speed, gradually alternate between adding the flour mixture and your buttermilk, starting and ending with the flour mixture. Stir until each one is almost completely combined before adding the next. Scrape the sides and bottom of the bowl so that all ingredients are combined.
7. In separate bowl, combine your egg whites and, with a hand-mixer on high-speed, beat until stiff peaks form.
8. Using a spatula, gently fold your egg whites and sprinkles into your batter. Scrape the sides and bottom of the bowl so that ingredients are well-combined, and take care not to over-mix.
9. Divide batter into prepared cupcake tin, filling each liner ¾ of the way full.
10. Bake on 350° F for 18 minutes, or until a toothpick inserted in the center comes out mostly clean with moist crumbs. For mini cupcakes, bake 14-15 minutes.
11. Allow cupcakes to cool completely before frosting.

VANILLA BUTTERCREAM

1. Beat butter with an electric mixer until creamy. Sprinkle salt over butter and stir again to combine.
2. Gradually, about ½ cup at a time, add powdered sugar, waiting until each cup is completely mixed before adding more.
3. With mixer on medium-low speed, add the heavy cream one tablespoon at a time. Once ingredients are well incorporated, gradually increase speed to high and beat for about 30 seconds.
4. Add vanilla extract and stir well.
5. Spread frosting over cooled cupcakes. Top with sprinkles.

TRADITIONAL BIRTHDAY CAKE

MAKES 8 SERVINGS

INGREDIENTS

CAKE

- 2 ¼ cups all-purpose flour
- 2 ¼ tsp baking powder
- ¾ tsp salt
- ¾ cup unsalted butter room temperature
- 1 ½ cup granulated sugar
- 3 large eggs room temperature
- 2 tsp good vanilla extract
- 1 cup whole milk (room temperature)

VANILLA FROSTING

- 1 cup unsalted butter softened to room temperature
- ¼ teaspoon salt
- 3 cups powdered sugar
- 3 tablespoons heavy cream
- 1 teaspoon vanilla extract

GARNISH

- birthday sprinkles

INSTRUCTIONS

VANILLA CAKE

1. Preheat oven to 350° F. Grease and flour two 8" cake rounds and line with parchment paper.

2. In a medium bowl, whisk flour, baking powder, and salt until well combined. Set aside.

3. Using a stand mixer fitted with a paddle attachment or a hand mixe, cream butter and sugar on med-high until pale and fluffy (3 mins). Reduce speed and add eggs one at a time fully incorporating after each addition. Add vanilla.

4. Alternate adding flour mixture and milk, beginning and ending with flour (3 additions of flour and 2 of milk). Fully incorporating after each addition.

5. Bake for 35-40 mins or until a toothpick inserted into the center comes out mostly clean.

VANILLA BUTTERCREAM

6. Beat butter with an electric mixer until creamy. Sprinkle salt over butter and stir again to combine.

7. Gradually, about ½ cup at a time, add powdered sugar, waiting until each cup is completely mixed before adding more.

8. With mixer on medium-low speed, add the heavy cream, one tablespoon at a time. Once ingredients are well incorporated, gradually increase speed to high and beat for about 30 seconds.

9. Add vanilla extract and stir well.

10. Pipe or spread frosting over cooled cakes. Top with sprinkles, if desired.

INGREDIENTS

CAKE POPS

- 1 and ⅔ cups all-purpose flour
- ½ teaspoon baking powder
- ¼ teaspoon baking soda
- ½ teaspoon salt
- ½ cup (1 stick) unsalted butter, softened to room temperature
- 1 cup granulated sugar
- 1 large egg, at room temperature
- 2 teaspoons pure vanilla extract
- 1 cup whole milk (or buttermilk)

FROSTING

- 7 tablespoons unsalted butter, softened to room temperature
- 1 ¾ cups confectioners' sugar
- 2-3 teaspoons heavy cream or milk
- 1 teaspoon pure vanilla extract

COATING

- 40 ounces pure white chocolate
- sprinkles

CAKE POPS

MAKES 12 SERVINGS

INSTRUCTIONS

1. Preheat oven to 350° F (177° C). Grease a 9-inch cake pan.

2. Whisk the flour, baking powder, baking soda, and salt together in a medium bowl. Set aside. Using a hand-held or stand mixer fitted with a paddle or whisk attachment, beat the butter and sugar together in a large bowl until creamed, about 2 minutes. Add the egg and vanilla extract and beat on high speed until combined. Scrape down the bottom and sides of the bowl as needed.

3. With the mixer running on low speed, add the dry ingredients and milk to the wet ingredients until combined. Manually whisk the batter to ensure there are no large lumps at the bottom of the bowl. Batter will be slightly thick. Pour the batter evenly into the prepared pan. Bake for 30-36 minutes or until a toothpick inserted in the center comes out clean. If the top begins browning too quickly in the oven, loosely place a piece of aluminum foil on top.

4. All the cake to cool completely in the pan set on a wire rack.

5. With a handheld or stand mixer fitted with a paddle attachment, beat the butter on medium speed until creamy, about 2 minutes. Add confectioners' sugar, heavy cream, and vanilla extract with the mixer running on low. Increase to high speed and beat for 3 full minutes.

6. Crumble the cooled cake into the bowl on top of the frosting. Make sure there are no large lumps. Turn the mixer on low and beat the frosting and cake crumbles together until combined.

7. Measure 1 tablespoon of moist cake mixture and roll into a ball. Place balls on a lined baking sheet. Refrigerate for 2 hours or freeze for 1 hour. Re-roll the chilled balls to smooth out, if needed. Place back into the fridge as you'll only work with a couple at a time.

8. Melt the coating in a 2-cup liquid measuring cup (best for dunking!). you can use a double boiler or microwave.

9. Remove only 2-3 cake balls from the refrigerator at a time. Dip a lollipop stick about ½ inch into the coating, then insert into the center or the cake ball. Only push it about halfway through the cake ball. Dip the cake ball into the coating until it is completely covered. Make sure the coating covers the base of the cake ball where it meets the lollipop stick. Very gently tap the stick against the edge of the measuring cup to allow excess coating to drop off. Decorate the top with sprinkles and place upright into a styrofoam block or box. Repeat with remaining cake balls, only working with some out of the refrigerator at a time. The cake balls must be very cold when dipping!

10. Coating will set within an hour. Store cake pops in the refrigerator for up to 1 week.

WAFFLE ICE CREAM SANDWICHES

MAKES 4 SERVINGS

INGREDIENTS

- 8 toasted waffles
- 4 cups of ice cream

PICK YOUR GARNISH

- decorative candies
- sprinkles
- crushed nuts
- toasted coconut

INSTRUCTIONS

1. If using peanut butter, fluff or preserves spread a thin layer on one waffle.
2. Place the ice cream on top of one waffle.
3. Top with another waffle.
4. Then roll the optional garnishes along sides of ice cream and enjoy.

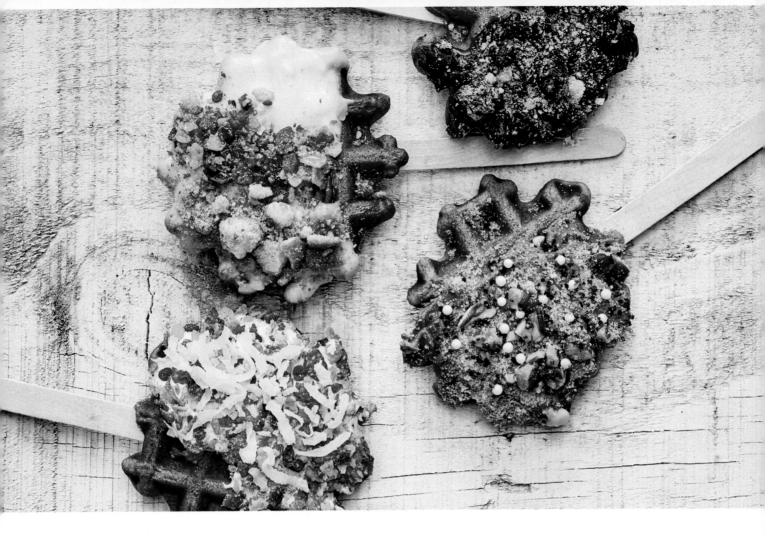

WAFFLE POPS

MAKES 16 SERVINGS

INGREDIENTS

- 4 toasted waffles
- 16 popsicle sticks

PICK YOUR GARNISH

- decorative candies
- sprinkles
- crushed nuts
- toasted coconut
- cereal
- cookies of your choice
- white chocolate (melted)

INSTRUCTIONS

1. Cut waffles into to 4 equal pieces.

2. To make confetti waffles: Drizzle waffles with melted white chocolate and top with sprinkles.

3. To make chocolate banana waffles: Drizzle waffles with melted peanut butter and garnish with mini chocolate chips and banana slices.

4. To make cookies 'n cream waffles: Drizzle waffles with melted chocolate and sprinkle with crushed Oreos.

5. Be creative and build your own.

CARROT CAKE

MAKES 8 SERVINGS

INGREDIENTS

CAKE

- butter, for pans
- 2 cups all-purpose flour, plus more for pans
- 2 cups sugar
- 2 teaspoons baking soda
- 2 teaspoons ground cinnamon
- 1 teaspoon salt
- 4 eggs
- 1 ½ cups vegetable oil
- 3 cups grated carrots
- 1 ½ cups chopped pecans, optional

FROSTING

- 2 8-ounce packages cream cheese, room temperature
- 1 stick salted butter, room temperature
- 1 16-ounce box powdered sugar
- 1 teaspoon vanilla extract
- ½ cup chopped pecans

INSTRUCTIONS

CAKE

1. Preheat oven to 350° F. Grease and flour 3 (9-inch) round pans; Line bottom of the pans with parchment paper.

2. In a large bowl, combine flour, sugar, baking soda, cinnamon, and salt. Add eggs and vegetable oil. Using a hand mixer, blend until combined. Add carrots and pecans, if using.

3. Pour into pans. Bake for approximately 40 minutes. Remove from oven and cool for 5 minutes. Remove from pans, place on waxed paper and allow to cool completely before frosting.

FROSTING

1. Add all ingredients, except nuts, into a medium bowl and beat until fluffy using a hand mixer. Stir in the nuts. Spread frosting on top of each cake layer. Stack the cakes on a serving plate and serve.

WAFFLE BREAD PUDDING

MAKES 6 SERVINGS

INGREDIENTS

BREAD PUDDING

- 3 eggs, beaten
- 1 ½ cups white sugar
- 2 tablespoons light brown sugar
- ½ teaspoon ground cinnamon
- ¼ cup butter, melted
- 2 cups half and half
- 6 cooked waffles cut into cubes

VANILLA SAUCE

- ½ cup light brown sugar
- 1 tablespoon all-purpose flour
- 1 pinch ground cinnamon
- 1 egg
- 2 tablespoons butter, melted
- 1 ¼ cups whole milk
- 1 pinch salt
- 1 tablespoon vanilla extract

INSTRUCTIONS

1. Preheat oven to 350° F. Grease a 2-quart baking dish.

2. In a mixing bowl, eggs, sugar, brown sugar, cinnamon, butter and milk together, and gently stir in the waffle cubes. Spoon the mixture into the baking dish.

3. Bake in the preheated oven until browned and set in the middle, 50 to 55 minutes; cover the dish with foil after 30 minutes to prevent excessive browning. Let the pudding stand for 10 minutes before serving.

4. For vanilla sauce, whisk brown sugar, flour, a pinch of cinnamon, egg, melted butter, milk, and salt together in a saucepan until smooth. Heat over medium heat, whisking constantly, until thickened 10 to 12 minutes. Stir in the vanilla extract. Pour sauce over warm bread pudding, or serve on the side in a bowl.

INGREDIENTS

NO BAKE CHEESECAKE

- 2 8 ounce packages of cream cheese
- ¾ cup granulated sugar
- 1 tablespoon fresh juice from 1 lemon
- 1 teaspoon vanilla extract
- ⅛ teaspoon kosher salt
- 1 ½ cups heavy whipping cream

CARROT CAKE

- 20 ounce peeled raw carrots
- ¾ cup unsalted butter, room temperature
- 1 ½ cups sugar
- ½ tsp vanilla extract
- 3 tbsp vegetable oil
- 3 large eggs
- 1 large egg white
- 2 ½ cups all-purpose flour
- 2 tsp baking powder

- 1 tsp baking soda
- ½ tsp salt
- 2 tsp ground cinnamon
- 1 tsp ginger
- ½ tsp nutmeg
- ⅛ tsp cloves
- ⅛ tsp all spice
- 8 ounce crushed pineapple, drained
- 1 cup sweetened coconut flakes

CARROT CAKE CHEESECAKE

MAKES 14-16 SERVINGS

INSTRUCTIONS

NO BAKE CHEESECAKE

1. Combine the cream cheese, sugar, lemon juice, vanilla, and salt in the bowl of a stand mixer fitted with a paddle attachment. Mix at medium speed until soft and smooth. Scrape the bowl as needed.

2. Switch to the whisk attachment and pour in the cream. Mix at low speed to combine, then increase to high and whip until the mixture can hold stiff peaks, 3 to 5 minutes.

3. Pour into the prepared crust.

4. Refrigerate until the filling is firm and cold, about 6 hours or overnight.

CARROT CAKE

5. To steam the carrots, bring about an inch of water to a boil in the bottom of a pot. Put peeled carrots in a steamer basket set over the boiling water. Cover and steam the carrots until very tender, about 10-15 minutes.

6. Put the warm carrots into a food processor and puree. You should end up with about 1 ¾ cup (420ml) of carrot puree. Set aside to cool.

7. Preheat the oven to 350° F. Line the bottom of two 9-inch cake pans with parchment paper and grease the sides.

8. In a large mixer bowl, cream the butter and sugar on medium speed until light in color and fluffy, 3-4 minutes.

9. Add vanilla extract and vegetable oil and mix until combined.

10. Add eggs one at a time, mixing until incorporated after each addition.

11. Add the egg white and mix until well combined. Scrape down the sides of the bowl as needed to make sure everything is combined.

12. Combine the dry ingredients in a medium sized bowl.

13. Add half of the flour mixture to the batter and mix until combined.

14. Add the carrot puree to the batter and mix until combined.

15. Add the remaining flour mixture and mix until well combined and smooth.

16. Stir in the crushed pineapple and coconut flakes. Scrape down the sides of the bowl as needed to ensure everything is well combined.

17. Divide the batter evenly between the prepared cake pans. Bake for 30-35 minutes, or until a toothpick inserted in the middle comes out with a few crumbs.

18. Remove cakes from the oven and allow to cool for 3-4 minutes, then remove from the pans to a cooling rack to finish cooling.

LAYERING CAKE

1. Use a large serrated knife to remove the domes from the top of the two carrot cakes.

2. Place the first layer of cake on a serving plate or a cardboard cake round.

3. Use the aluminum foil to lift the cheesecake out of the cake pan, remove the foil and place the cheesecake on top of the cake.

4. Add the second layer of cake on top. If the sides of the cake don't line up, use a serrated knife to trim off the excess cake or cheesecake.

5. Press the pecans into the sides of the cake

6. Finish off the cake with some candy carrots or other carrot decor.

GINGERBREAD POUND CAKE

MAKES 12 SERVINGS

INGREDIENTS

- 1 cup softened butter or 1 cup margarine
- 1 cup sugar
- 5 eggs
- 2 cups all-purpose flour
- ½ teaspoon baking soda
- 1 teaspoon ground ginger
- 1 teaspoon ground cinnamon
- 1 teaspoon ground cloves
- 1 cup molasses
- ½ cup sour cream
- sifted powdered sugar

INSTRUCTIONS

1. In a mixing bowl, cream butter beating well on medium speed with an electric mixer; gradually add sugar.

2. Add eggs, one at a time, beating after each egg is added.

3. Combine flour, soda, and spices; set aside.

4. Combine molasses and sour cream.

5. Add flour mixture to creamed mixture alternately with molasses mixture, beginning and ending with flour mixture.

6. Mix just until blended after each addition.

7. Pour batter into a greased and floured 10-inch Bundt pan.

8. Bake at 325° F for 1 hour or until wooden pick inserted in center comes out clean.

9. Cool in pan for 15 minutes then remove and cool completely on a wire cake rack.

10. Sprinkle with powdered sugar.

SALTED CARAMEL MILK SHAKE

MAKES 4 SERVINGS

INGREDIENTS

SHAKE

- 4 scoops packed vanilla bean ice cream
- ½ cup whole milk
- 3 tablespoons salted caramel syrup
- 4 tablespoons of vanilla frosting

GARNISHES

- sweet potato waffles
- pretzel sticks
- whipped cream
- crushed graham cracker crumbs
- caramel syrup

INSTRUCTIONS

1. Place ice cream, milk, caramel syrup into and blender.
2. Blend on medium-high speed until thoroughly combined.
3. Coat rim of glass with vanilla frosting, then roll the rim of glass with crushed graham cracker crumbs.
4. Pour milk shake into a glass. Top with mini sweet potato waffles and garnishes.

RED VELVET FUNNEL CAKE

MAKES 4 SERVINGS

INGREDIENTS

- 4 cups vegetable or canola oil for frying
- 2 cups all-purpose flour
- 3 tablespoons granulated sugar
- 1 tablespoon cocoa powder
- 1 ½ teaspoon baking powder
- ½ teaspoon salt
- 1 ½ cups milk
- 2 large eggs
- 1 teaspoon pure vanilla extract
- 3 tablespoons red food coloring
- confectioner's sugar

INSTRUCTIONS

1. Heat oil in a pot to about 375° F.

2. In a bowl, whisk together flour, sugar, cocoa powder, baking powder, and salt until combined.

3. Then whisk in wet ingredients: milk, eggs and vanilla extract until the batter is nice and smooth. Add red food coloring as well and whisk until all of the batter is red.

4. Add batter squeeze bottle and cut the tip of bottle.

5. Once oil is nice and hot, swirl batter in a spirally shape into the oil and fry. Turn over once the first side is nice and golden brown.

6. Once both sides are golden brown, remove from oil and place on paper towels to drain. These babies fry fast!

7. Immediately cover with confectioner's sugar or other toppings and serve while hot.

COUNTRY LEMONADE

MAKES 8 SERVINGS

INGREDIENTS

- 6 cups filtered water
- 7 juiced lemons
- 1 cup sugar
- mint leaves (for garnish)
- fresh fruit

INSTRUCTIONS

1. In a pitcher combine lemon juice and water. Stir in sugar until dissolved.
2. Garnish with mint leaves and fresh fruit.
3. Pour into glasses filled with ice and serve.

PEACH SWEET TEA

MAKES 8 SERVINGS

INGREDIENTS

- 3 peaches (diced into small pieces)
- 5 cups water
- 2 ½ cups granulated sugar
- 1 juiced lemon
- 3 family sized tea bags
- mint leaves (for garnish)

INSTRUCTIONS

1. In a saucepan combine peaches, sugar and 2 cups of water.
2. Allow to simmer for 15 minutes.
3. With a blender, pulse for 15-30 seconds until mixture becomes smooth.
4. Strain the peach mixture through a small strainer, extracting only the syrup
5. Boil 3 cups of water.
6. After water is at boiling point, steep 3 bags of tea in the boiling water for 15 minutes.
7. Pour tea mixture and peach mixture into a pitcher and stir. Taste for sweetness.
8. If more sugar is needed add ½ cup of granulated sugar at a time until perfectly sweet.
9. Serve over a full glass of ice and garnish with ice.

HOMEMADE FRUIT PUNCH

MAKES 8 SERVINGS

INGREDIENTS

- 2 (6-ounce) cans frozen orange juice concentrate, thawed
- 2 (6-ounce) cans frozen lemonade concentrate, thawed
- 1 (48-ounce) can pineapple juice
- 3 cups water
- 1 ½ cups granulated sugar
- 1 juiced lemon
- 1 bottle of lemon-lime soda
- fresh fruit for garnish

INSTRUCTIONS

1. Combine the orange juice, lemonade, and pineapple juice and stir well.

2. Bring 3 cups water and the sugar to a boil in a heavy saucepan and boil until sugar is dissolved, about 5 minutes. Let cool. Add the syrup to the fruit juices.

3. When ready to serve, pour the fruit juice into a pitcher and add the soda.

ARNOLD PALMER

MAKES 8 SERVINGS

INGREDIENTS

- ice cubes
- 1 cup black tea (see peach iced tea recipe)
- ¾ lemonade (see lemonade recipe)
- lemon round, for garnish

INSTRUCTIONS

1. Fill a tall glass with ice. Add the tea and lemonade and stir to combine. Garnish with the lemon round and drink immediately.

JALAPEÑO CHEDDAR CORNBREAD

MAKES 6-8 SERVINGS

INGREDIENTS

- 1 ¼ cup all-purpose flour
- 1 cup + 3 tablespoons of Best Yellow Cornmeal (Dixie Lily)
- 1 cup sugar
- 1 tablespoon baking powder
- 1 teaspoon salt
- 1 ¼ cup milk
- 2 eggs
- ¼ tablespoon butter
- 1 cup shredded cheddar
- 1 diced jalapeño
- ½ cup fresh corn
- 1 tablespoon fresh green onion

INSTRUCTIONS

1. Preheat oven to 350° F.
2. Combine flour, cornmeal, sugar, baking powder and salt in a large bowl.
3. Then add milk, eggs and melted butter to dry mixture. Gently stir until combined.
4. Add shredded cheddar, jalapeño, fresh corn and green onion in bowl with cornbread mixture and stir again.
5. Coat cast iron skillet or 12 count muffin pan with shortening or spray with non-stick baking spray until fully covered. Add cornbread mixture to skillet.
6. Place in oven for 25 minutes until cornbread is done. Remove from oven and serve.

SOUTHERN HUSHPUPPIES

MAKES 4 SERVINGS

INGREDIENTS

- 1 cup yellow cornmeal
- 1 cup self-rising flour
- ½ tsp salt
- ½ tsp cayenne pepper
- 2 tbsp granulated sugar
- 1 tsp garlic powder
- 1 small onion finely diced
- 3-4 green onions thinly diced
- 1 cup buttermilk
- 1 large egg
- 2 cup of oil for deep frying

INSTRUCTIONS

1. Combine the cornmeal, self-rising flour, sugar, salt, cayenne pepper, and garlic in a large bowl.
2. Whisk until everything is lump free then toss in the diced onions.
3. Add in the buttermilk and egg.
4. Mix the ingredients until well combined, but don't over mix.
5. Pour the oil into a large pan, and heat the oil over medium heat.
6. Once the oil is hot, spoon batter with a small ice cream scoop
7. Fry the hush puppies until they are golden brown.
8. Remove the hush puppies from the oil, and place them on a paper towel lined plate.

CRAB STUFFED SHRIMP AND GRIT CAKES

MAKES 4 SERVINGS

INGREDIENTS

GRIT CAKES

- 5 cups water
- dash of salt (or to taste)
- 1 cup stone ground grits
- ¼ cup heavy cream
- 2 large eggs
- ½ cup Italian bread crumbs
- vegetable oil (for frying)

CRAB STUFFED SHRIMP

- 2 eggs, lightly beaten
- Italian breadcrumbs
- 2 tablespoons light mayonnaise
- 1 teaspoon lemon juice
- ½ teaspoon old bay
- ½ teaspoon black pepper
- ⅛ teaspoon cayenne pepper
- 1 lb lump crabmeat
- 1 lb large shrimp

LEMON CREAM SAUCE

- ¼ teaspoon butter
- ¾ cup cream
- 1 lemon
- ¼ cup white wine
- salt
- pepper

INSTRUCTIONS

GRIT CAKES

1. Bring the water and salt to a boil in a large heavy saucepan.
2. Add the grits and continue to simmer, stirring constantly, over medium heat until the grits are cooked and thick like mush, about 30 to 40 minutes. Add cream and stir. Season with salt and pepper to taste.
3. Pour the hot grits onto a large plate to make a layer about ¾-inch deep. Cover and let stand to cool, then refrigerate to chill thoroughly.
4. When the grits are cold and firm, cut them into rectangular pieces or use biscuit cutters and cut rounds.
5. Crack eggs and whisk in bowl.
6. Dredge the grits pieces in bread crumbs, shaking off any excess bread crumbs.
7. Heat about ½-inch of vegetable oil in a large, heavy skillet over medium-high heat. Fry the grits cakes until golden brown on both sides, about 4 to 5 minutes total.
8. Drain on paper towels and sprinkle with salt.
9. Serve hot.

CRAB STUFFED SHRIMP

1. Peel shrimp leaving tails and slice down middle deveining as you go.
2. Lay on greased cookie sheet to form a circle with the tail pointing up.
3. (Fan the tail out for beauty and handle.) Mix first 7 ingredients and gently fold into crabmeat.
4. Place a spoonful of crabmeat mixture on top of the circle.
5. Place cookie sheet in 350° F oven for 15 minutes, remove with spatula to serving tray. Serve immediately.

LEMON CREAM SAUCE

1. In sauté pan melt butter, then add cream, lemon, white wine.
2. Reduce for 3-4 minutes, then add salt and pepper to taste.

CAJUN CHICKEN EGG ROLLS

MAKES 6 SERVINGS

INGREDIENTS

- 1 cup corn kernels
- 1 cup black beans
- ¼ cup sliced green onions
- ¼ cup seeded and minced jalapeño pepper
- 2 cups shredded Monterey Jack cheese
- 1 ½ cups cooked diced chicken breast
- 1 tablespoon old bay
- 1 package egg roll wrappers
- oil for frying
- Creole Ranch
- ½ cup ranch dressing
- 1 tablespoon hot sauce
- 1 teaspoon old bay

INSTRUCTIONS

1. In a large bowl mix together the corn, beans, jalapeño pepper, green onion, cheese, diced chicken breast and old bay.

2. Place one egg roll wrapper on a cutting board. Place 2 heaping tablespoons onto the wrapper and roll up according to package directions, sealing the edge with a little water.

3. Repeat the process with the remaining filling and egg roll wrappers.

4. Place the egg rolls on a parchment lined sheet pan. Cover and freeze for at least 2 hours, or up to a month.

5. Heat a large skillet over medium high heat. Pour oil into the pan until a depth of 1-inch is reached.

6. Place 4-5 egg rolls in the pan, do not overcrowd. Cook for 3-4 minutes per side or until deep golden brown, then drain on paper towels. Repeat the process with the remaining egg rolls.

7. While the egg rolls are frying, make the dipping sauce. In a small bowl combine ranch, hot sauce and old bay.

8. Cut the egg rolls in half on the diagonal and serve immediately with ranch dressing for dipping.

PETIT BISCUITS

MAKES 12-16 SERVINGS

INGREDIENTS

- 2 cups unbleached white flour
- 1 tablespoon baking powder
- 1 teaspoon baking soda
- ¼ teaspoon kosher salt
- 1 tablespoon sugar
- 1 ½ cup of buttermilk or ¾ cups of milk
- 6 tablespoons butter

INSTRUCTIONS

1. Preheat oven to 400° F.
2. Place flour, baking powder, baking soda, salt and sugar into a bowl.
3. Dice cold butter into small chunks.
4. Place butter into dry mixture and incorporate into flour until it resembles a coarse crumbs.
5. Add milk to dry mixture, stir just until combined.
6. Batter should look wet, if it appears dry, add more milk.

DROP BISCUITS

7. Take tablespoon or ice cream scoop and scoop onto a greased baking sheet
8. Bake on 400° F for 10-15 minutes.

TRADITIONAL SOUTHERN BISCUITS

9. Turn the dough out onto a lightly floured surface.
10. Fold the dough about 10 times.
11. Gently, roll or pat the dough out until it's about 1 inch thick.
12. Take biscuit cutter and cut biscuits. Place onto a greased or non-stick baking sheet.
13. Place about ¾ inches apart for crusty sides or close together for softer sides.
14. Bake for 10-15 minutes until golden brown.

ONION RINGS

MAKES 8 SERVINGS

INGREDIENTS

- Mama's Fried Chicken Coating (see page 51)
- 2 onions, sliced into half inch onion rings
- 1 cup of buttermilk
- vegetable oil for frying

INSTRUCTIONS

1. Dip each onion ring into Mama's Fried Chicken Coating then dip into buttermilk then back into seasoned flour coating all sides. Set each battered onion ring on a parchment covered baking sheet to rest until all onion rings are battered.

2. While coating sets, add 3 inches of oil to a cast iron or heavy bottom pot and heat over medium high heat. Also turn on oven to 275 degrees.

3. Fry onion rings a few at a time. Fry on each side until golden brown then remove and place on paper towels to drain.

4. Add finished onion rings to a parchment paper lined baking sheet or paper towel.

FRIED LOBSTER DEVILED EGGS

MAKES 6 SERVINGS

INGREDIENTS

DEVILED EGGS

- 6 large eggs
- 2 tablespoons mayonnaise
- 1 ½ tablespoons sweet pickle relish
- 1 teaspoon prepared mustard
- ⅛ teaspoon salt
- dash of pepper

GARNISH

- paprika

FRIED LOBSTER

- 2 lobster tails
- 1 egg
- ¼ cup water
- 2 cups Mama's Fried Chicken Coating (see page 51)
- 3 cups vegetable oil

INSTRUCTIONS

FOR DEVILED EGGS

1. Place eggs in a single layer in a saucepan; add water to depth of 3 inches. Bring to a boil; cover, remove from heat, and let stand 15 minutes.

2. Drain immediately and fill the saucepan with cold water and ice. Tap each egg firmly on the counter until cracks form all over the shell. Peel under cold running water.

3. Slice eggs in half lengthwise, and carefully remove yolks. Mash yolks with mayonnaise. Add relish, mustard, salt, and pepper; stir well. Spoon yolk mixture into egg whites. Garnish, if desired.

FRIED LOBSTER TAILS

1. Place oil in a skillet on medium heat or 350° F with a candy thermometer.

2. Beat eggs and water. Set aside.

3. Mix together Mama's Fried Chicken Coating in a large bowl.

4. Cut the lobster tail down the middle and remove meat. Cut the meat into big bite sized chunks. Dip into egg wash coating well. Then dip into Mama's Fried Chicken Coating. Deep fry a few pieces at a time for 3-4 minutes.

5. Cook until golden brown, then place on a lined paper towel.

ASSEMBLY

1. Place deviled eggs on a serving tray.

2. Top with a piece of fried lobster.

TIP: *Drizzle honey hot sauce over the top (recipe in bonus section).*

CANDIED BACON DEVILED EGGS

MAKES 6 SERVINGS

INGREDIENTS

DEVILED EGGS

- 6 large eggs
- 2 tablespoons mayonnaise
- 1 ½ tablespoons sweet pickle relish
- 1 teaspoon sugar
- 1 teaspoon prepared mustard
- ⅛ teaspoon salt
- dash of pepper

GARNISH

- paprika

CANDIED BACON

- follow recipe on page 14

INSTRUCTIONS

DEVILED EGGS

1. Place eggs in a single layer in a saucepan; add water to depth of 3 inches. Bring to a boil; cover, remove from heat, and let stand 15 minutes.

2. Drain immediately and fill the saucepan with cold water and ice. Tap each egg firmly on the counter until cracks form all over the shell. Peel under cold running water.

3. Slice eggs in half lengthwise, and carefully remove yolks. Mash yolks with mayonnaise. Add relish, mustard, salt, sugar and pepper; stir well. Spoon yolk mixture into egg whites. Garnish, if desired.

CANDIED BACON

1. Chopped finished candied bacon into small pieces.

ASSEMBLY

1. Place deviled eggs on a serving tray.
2. Top with a piece of candied bacon.

FRIED CHICKEN WAFFLE BENEDICT

MAKES 4 SERVINGS

INGREDIENTS

- 2 chicken breasts, pounded to even thickness and cut in half
- 3 cups of vegetable oil
- 1 cup of Mama's Fried Chicken Coating (see page 51)
- 6 eggs
- 2 cooked waffles (see page 6)

FOR HOLLANDAISE

- 3 large egg yolks
- 1 tablespoon lemon juice
- ½ cup firm butter
- 4 eggs for frying

INSTRUCTIONS

1. Preheat skillet with oil to medium heat or 350° F with a candy thermometer.

2. Crack 2 eggs in a shallow bowl and whisk.

3. Place Mama's Fried Chicken Coating in a shallow dish.

4. Dredge the chicken breast in egg wash mixture and then in coating. Shake off excess coating. Then place in a skillet and cook 3-4 minutes on each side. Allow to drain on a plate lined with paper towels.

5. To make the hollandaise, add 3 egg yolks and lemon juice to a blender. Pulse to combine. Melt butter in small saucepan. Set blender to low and slowly add melted butter while it is running. Continue to blend until sauce is thick and frothy. Season with salt and pepper.

6. To build, place waffle on serving dish. Place one piece of fried chicken on each half and top with a fried egg to your liking. Drizzle with hollandaise right before serving.

CRISPY FISH TACOS

MAKES 4 SERVINGS

INGREDIENTS

TACOS

- 1 pound catfish or red snapper
- canola oil
- 1 egg
- Mama's Fried Chicken Coating (see page 51)
- 8 flour tortillas

GARNISH

- shredded white cabbage
- sour cream
- thinly sliced red onion
- hot sauce
- jalapeño

INSTRUCTIONS

1. Preheat canola oil to medium heat in frying pan.

2. Place egg in a bowl and whisk.

3. Dredge fish in egg and then dredge in Mama's Fried Chicken Coating.

4. Fry for 2 minutes on each side or until golden brown.

5. Line a baking sheet with paper towels and place fish on the baking sheet.

6. Place the tortillas in a frying pan for 20 seconds. Divide the fish among the tortillas and garnish with any or all of the garnishes.

PULLED PORK BISCUITS

MAKES 4 SERVINGS

INGREDIENTS

PULLED PORK

- 1 cup water
- 1 tablespoon packed dark brown sugar
- ½ teaspoon granulated garlic
- 1 tablespoon kosher salt, plus more as needed
- ½ teaspoon black pepper
- 1 (4 ½ to 5-pound) boneless or bone-in pork shoulder (also known as pork butt)
- 2 cups of your favorite barbecue sauce

SLAW

- ½ head green cabbage, finely shredded
- ½ head red cabbage, finely shredded
- 2 large carrots, finely shredded
- ½ red onion, finely sliced
- ¾ cup mayonnaise
- 3 tablespoons distilled vinegar
- 2 tablespoons sugar
- salt and freshly ground black pepper
- hot biscuits (see biscuit recipe)

INSTRUCTIONS

PULLED PORK

1. Combine the sugar, pepper and granulated garlic in a small bowl. Pat the pork dry with paper towels. Rub the spice mixture all over the pork and place in the crockpot. Cover and cook until the pork is fork tender, about 6 to 8 hours on high or 8 to 10 hours on low.

2. Turn off the slow cooker and remove the pork

3. Using 2 forks, shred the meat into bite-sized pieces, discarding any large pieces of fat. Return the shredded meat to the slow cooker, add the barbecue sauce, if using, and mix to combine.

SLAW

1. Combine the red and green cabbage, carrots and red onions in a large bowl. Whisk together the mayonnaise, cider vinegar, sugar, and some salt and pepper in a medium bowl, and then add to the cabbage mixture.

2. Mix well to combine.

3. Taste for seasoning; adjust with more salt, pepper or sugar as needed.

4. Assemble biscuit with pulled pork and slaw. Enjoy.

SOUTHERN FRIED CHICKEN

MAKES 4 SERVINGS

INGREDIENTS

- 1-lb of chicken
- 2 eggs
- ½ cup water
- 2 cups Mama's Fried Chicken Coating (see below)
- 3 cups of vegetable or peanut oil

INSTRUCTIONS

1. Heat oil in a large skillet on medium heat or 350° F.

2. In a large bowl crack two eggs and ½ cup water. Whisk the both together.

3. Place Mama's Fried Chicken Coating in a shallow dish.

4. Dip chicken in egg wash and then in Mama's Fried Chicken Coating. Be sure to shake of excess flour mixture.

5. Place in hot skillet and cook dark pieces 6-8 minutes and white pieces 12-14 minutes. Chicken will be golden brown and float to the top of skillet when completely done.

SOUTHERN FRIED CHICKEN WITH MAMA'S FRIED CHICKEN COATING

MAKES 6 SERVINGS

INGREDIENTS

- 2 cups flour
- ½ cup corn starch
- ¾ cup salt
- ⅛ cup black pepper
- ⅛ cup paprika
- ¼ cup granulated garlic
- ¼ cup onion
- ⅛ cup cayenne

INSTRUCTIONS

1. Combine all ingredients and store in an air tight container for up to 6 months.

CHICKEN AND SHRIMP SKILLET POT PIE

MAKES 6 SERVINGS

INGREDIENTS

- 6 hot baked biscuits (see biscuit recipe)
- 1 tbsp olive oil
- 2 boneless, skinless chicken breasts, diced
- ½ lb large shrimp
- kosher salt
- ground black pepper
- ½ onion, chopped
- 2 medium carrots, peeled and chopped
- 2 stalks celery, chopped
- 1 large potato (diced)
- 3 tbsp flour
- 1 ½ cups frozen peas
- ½ cup chicken broth
- 1 ½ cups heavy cream

INSTRUCTIONS

1. In a large skillet over medium-heat, heat oil. Add chicken and season with salt and pepper. Cook until browned on all sides and remove from skillet.

2. Add shrimp and season with salt and pepper. Cook for 3 minutes and set aside.

3. Add onion, carrots, celery, and potatoes and cook until vegetables are soft, 6-8 minutes.

4. Sprinkle flour over vegetables and cook 2-3 minutes more.

5. Add chicken broth and bring to a simmer, cooking 8-10 minutes more, until slightly thickened.

6. Stir in cream, peas, and chicken and cook for 3-4 until cream has thicken.

7. Top with 4-6 hot biscuits and serve.

COUNTRY FRIED STEAK BITES

MAKES 4 SERVINGS

INGREDIENTS

STEAKS

- 1 Cup of Mama's Fried Chicken Coating (see page 51)
- 4 cubed steaks, sliced into strips
- 1 ½ cups milk
- 3 large eggs
- oil for frying

GRAVY

- ¼ cup onions
- 3 tablespoons Mama's Fried Chicken Coating
- ½ cup milk
- 1 ½ cups chicken stock

INSTRUCTIONS

STEAKS

1. In a bowl, whisk eggs and milk.
2. To another bowl, Mama's Fried Chicken Coating.
3. Place steaks to milk mixture.
4. Dip steak bites, one at a time, into coating each side then back into marinade then back into seasoned flour then finally place on a baking sheet.
5. Add oil to skillet or frying pan and heat over medium high heat.
6. Once oil is hot and ready, fry each steak bite on each side until golden brown. Drain on paper towels.

GRAVY

1. Add ¼ cup of the oil from frying to a skillet over medium.
2. Add in onions and cook for 2 minutes while stirring.
3. Next stir in Mama's Fried Chicken Coating.
4. Stir in milk and stock and turn heat up to high heat until boiling then turn heat down to medium low and allow to thicken.
5. Turn off heat. Place gravy into a ramekin and use for dipping country fried steak bites.

FRIED GREEN TOMATO PO BOY

MAKES 4 SERVINGS

INGREDIENTS

- Mama's Fried Chicken Coating (see page 51)
- 2 cups canola oil
- 3 large green tomatoes, cut into ¼-inch-thick slices
- 1 cup buttermilk
- 9 slices bacon
- 3 center split deli rolls
- 6 tablespoons mayonnaise
- 1 cup shredded romaine lettuce

INSTRUCTIONS

1. 1. Place Mama's Fried Chicken Coating in a shallow dish.

2. 2. Heat oil in a large skillet over medium-high heat. Dip tomato slices in buttermilk, and dredge in Mama's Fried Chicken Coating. Fry tomatoes, in batches, 2 minutes on each side or until golden. Drain on paper towels; set aside.

3. Heat bacon according to package directions; keep warm.

4. Split rolls and arrange, split sides up, on a baking sheet. Broil 5 inches from heat 2 minutes or until lightly toasted; remove from oven.

5. Spread cut sides of rolls with mayonnaise; place fried green tomatoes on bottom roll halves. Top with bacon and lettuce; sprinkle with hot sauce, if desired. Top with remaining roll halves, and serve immediately.

TRUFFLE SEA SALT BISCUITS

MAKES 12-16 SERVINGS

INGREDIENTS

- 2 cups unbleached white flour
- 1 tablespoon baking powder
- 1 teaspoon baking soda
- 1 teaspoon truffle sea salt
- 1 tablespoon sugar
- 1 ½ cups of buttermilk or ¾ cup of milk
- 6 tablespoons butter

INSTRUCTIONS

1. Preheat Oven to 400° F.
2. Place flour, baking powder, baking soda, truffle sea salt and sugar into a bowl.
3. Dice cold butter into small chunks.
4. Place butter into dry mixture and incorporate into flour until it resembles a coarse crumbs.
5. Add milk to dry mixture and stir just until combined.
6. Batter should look wet, if it appears dry, add more milk.

DROP BISCUITS

1. Take tablespoon or ice cream scoop and scoop onto a greased baking sheet
2. Bake on 400° F for 10-15 minutes.

TRADITIONAL SOUTHERN BISCUITS

1. Turn the dough out onto a lightly floured surface.
2. Fold the dough about 10 times.
3. Gently, roll or pat the dough out until it's about 1 inch thick.
4. Take biscuit cutter and cut biscuits. Place onto a greased or non-stick baking sheet.
5. Place about ¾ inches apart for crusty sides or close together for softer sides.
6. Bake for 10-15 minutes until golden brown.

SOUTHERN FRIED GRIT CAKES

MAKES 8 SERVINGS

INGREDIENTS

- 4 cups water
- dash of salt (or to taste)
- 1 cup stone ground grits
- ¼ cup cream
- ¼ cup butter
- ½ cup all-purpose flour
- vegetable oil (for frying)

INSTRUCTIONS

1. Bring the water and salt to a boil in a large heavy saucepan.

2. Add the grits and continue to simmer, stirring constantly, over medium heat until the grits are cooked and thick like mush, about 15 to 20 minutes. Add cream, butter, salt and pepper. If necessary, add a little more boiling water.

3. Pour the hot grits onto a baking sheet to make a layer about ¾-inch deep. Cover and let stand to cool, then refrigerate to chill thoroughly.

4. When the grits are cold and firm, cut them into rectangular pieces or use biscuit cutters and cut rounds.

5. Dredge the grits pieces with flour, shaking off any excess flour.

6. Heat about ½-inch of vegetable oil in a large, heavy skillet over medium-high heat. Fry the grits cakes until golden brown on both sides, about 4 to 5 minutes total.

7. Drain on paper towels and sprinkle with salt.

MAMA'S SWEET
ALABAMA CORNBREAD

MAKES 6 SERVINGS

INGREDIENTS

- 1 ¼ cup all-purpose flour
- 1 cup + 3 tablespoons of Best Yellow Cornmeal (Dixie Lily)
- 1 cup sugar
- 1 tablespoon baking powder
- 1 teaspoon salt
- ¼ cup butter (melted)
- 2 large eggs
- 1 ¼ cup of buttermilk or 1 cup milk

INSTRUCTIONS

1. Preheat oven to 350° F.
2. Combine flour, cornmeal, sugar, baking powder and salt in a large bowl.
3. Add milk, eggs and melted butter to dry mixture.
4. Once mixture is combined pour into a greased baking dish, 9-inch skillet (I like cast iron).
5. Bake for 25 minutes until golden brown.
6. Once out of the oven, brush melted butter.

SOUTHERN LOBSTER ROLLS

MAKES 4-6 SERVINGS

INGREDIENTS

- 4 cups cooked lobster meat, roughly 6 lobster tails (make sure meat is still warm)
- ½ cup good mayonnaise
- 1 teaspoon Dijon mustard
- ¼ cup thinly sliced green onions
- 1 tablespoon fresh lemon juice
- 1 tablespoon chopped celery
- 1 teaspoon old bay
- dash hot sauce
- 4-6 split top hot dog buns

INSTRUCTIONS

1. Butter and toast hot dog buns.

2. Combine lobster, mayo, mustard, celery, green onion, old bay and lemon juice and hot sauce together. Gently bring ingredients together. Spoon ¾ cup of lobster into each bun.

BLACKENED CATFISH

MAKES 4 SERVINGS

INGREDIENTS

CATFISH

- 4 catfish fillets or skinless fillets of other fish
- ½ cup melted butter
- ½ cup Cajun seasoning

CAJUN SEASONING

- 1 teaspoon black pepper
- ½ to 1 teaspoon cayenne pepper
- 1 teaspoon celery seed
- 2 tablespoons sweet paprika
- 1 tablespoon garlic powder
- 1 tablespoon dried thyme
- 1 tablespoon dried oregano

INSTRUCTIONS

1. In a large skillet, turn stove to medium high heat. Let the frying pan get hot for a good 3-4 minutes.

2. While the pan is heating up, melt the butter and pour the Cajun spices into a shallow dish.

3. Dip the fish fillets in the melted butter, then dredge in the Cajun spices. Shake off any excess. Lay the fish down on the hot pan.

4. Let the fish cook for 2-3 minutes. Using a wide metal spatula, carefully flip the catfish fillets and cook on the other side for another 2-3 minutes.

5. Serve and enjoy.

GARLIC PARMESAN GRITS

MAKES 6 SERVINGS

INGREDIENTS

- 3 ½ cups water
- 1 teaspoon salt
- 1 cup stone ground grits
- 4 to 6 tablespoons unsalted butter
- 1 cup heavy cream
- ½ cup shaved parmesan cheese
- ¼ teaspoon cracked black pepper
- 1 teaspoon granulated garlic
- ½ teaspoon sugar

INSTRUCTIONS

1. Add 3 ½ cups of water to a medium saucepan. Add salt and bring it to a boil over high heat.
2. Gradually stir in stone-ground grits.
3. Continue stirring and reduce the heat to low. Cook, stirring frequently, for about 40 to 50 minutes, or until the grits are very thick. Depending on the grind, cooking can take longer. As the grits thicken, they can scorch easily, so be sure to stir often. If the grits absorb all of the water before they are done, add more hot water as needed.
4. Beat in butter, cream, cheese, garlic, sugar and freshly ground black pepper.
5. Serve the grits hot.

GARLIC AND LEMON SHRIMP

MAKES 6 SERVINGS

INGREDIENTS

- ⅓ cup butter, divided
- 4 cloves garlic, minced (or 1 tablespoon)
- 1 pound shrimp, peeled and deveined, tails intact
- kosher salt and freshly ground black pepper, to taste
- juice of half a lemon (about 2 tablespoons)
- fresh chopped parsley, to garnish

INSTRUCTIONS

1. Melt 2 tablespoon butter in a large skillet over medium-high heat. Add the garlic and cook until fragrant (about 1 minute).
2. Fry shrimp and add salt and pepper, to your taste. Cook 2 minutes on one side, while stirring occasionally. Add the garlic and cook until fragrant (about 1 minute).
3. Flip and cook 2 minutes on the other side until JUST beginning to turn pink.
4. Add in the remaining butter and lemon juice. Cook, while stirring, until the butter melts and the shrimp have cooked through (do not overcook them). Take off heat. Taste test, and add more lemon juice, salt or pepper, if needed to suit your tastes.

COUNTRY GIRL SAUCE

MAKES 8 SERVINGS

INGREDIENTS

- 1 ¼ cup mayonnaise
- ¼ cup water
- 1 teaspoon ketchup
- 1 tablespoon melted butter
- ½ teaspoon garlic powder
- ½ teaspoon onion powder
- 1 teaspoon Worcestershire sauce
- 1 teaspoon sugar
- ¼ teaspoon paprika
- ½ teaspoon dried parsley

INSTRUCTIONS

1. Mix ingredients together. Cover and refrigerate overnight.
2. Make sure to refrigerate at least 4 hours.

HONEY HOT SAUCE DRIZZLE

MAKES 8 SERVINGS

INGREDIENTS

- ½ cup honey
- ¼ cup sriracha hot sauce

INSTRUCTIONS

1. Mix ingredients together. Place in a clear squeeze bottle and label.
2. Drizzle on whatever you like.

TURNED UP MAC AND CHEESE

MAKES 12 SERVINGS

INGREDIENTS

- 1 lb dried elbow pasta or pasta of your choice
- 1 stick butter
- 2 eggs
- 2 cups cup heavy whipping cream
- 3 cups grated or shaved Parmesan cheese
- 3 cups Monterey jack and mild cheddar cheese
- ½ tbsp salt
- ½ tsp black pepper
- 1 teaspoon sugar
- 1 teaspoon dried parsley

INSTRUCTIONS

1. Preheat over to 350° F.
2. Bring a large pot of water to the boil. Add macaroni and cook per packet directions.
3. Drain and add pasta to large mixing bowl.
4. Now add butter and heavy cream, salt, pepper and sugar. Mix well.
5. Then add 2 eggs, Parmesan cheese and ½ of Monterey Jack and cheddar. Reserve the rest for topping. Mix again.
6. Then top with remaining cheese and dried parsley
7. Place in oven for 25-30 minutes.